What I Like

We all are unique. We have different wishes, wants, needs and desires. It's what makes us who we are. Our spouses, children, and other family and friends have loved us for our uniqueness. What happens when we are no longer able to communicate these wants? You may already be blessed to have someone in your life who can express all your likes and dislikes but do they really know everything? This book is for you to help your loved ones hear your needs during a time when you cannot share with them directly. It is a guide for their benefit so they know how to help you.

Fill in the blanks with your likes and dislikes. There is a page for comments and room to answer your special questions that are not in the book. You are a human being until your last breath and it is important for people to continue to treat you like you. Be honest! Sharing things like, "I hate being called honey and sweetie and might be a bit combative with you if you disrespect me that way." It sounds impolite, but comments like this will help your caregiver to understand you better and enable you to have a much happier and much smoother relationship. Go into as much detail as you are comfortable with on the good and the bad. Our unpleasant experiences shape us as much as the good ones do. When we can't communicate verbally we usually do so with body language and caregivers need to know what makes you uncomfortable This improves the quality of life for everyone involved and can better meet your needs. It helps give your continuing life journey meaning.

As a professional case manager and caregiver support specialist, I began this journey by asking many people the question, what would you want someone to know if you could no longer communicate your needs? I received a diversity of answers. Some of these are listed here so you might have a better idea of the wide variety of things you can make sure people know.

My favorite season, to be outside, is the fall.

My favorite cereal is Raisin Bran.

I like my coffee with 2 teaspoons of coconut sugar and a couple of creams. Never plain.

I like my face to feel very clean.

I don't like raisins or fish.

Don't take me to the zoo or the circus.

Don't put Duck Dynasty on the TV. I hate that show.

I can't stand to sleep with socks on.

Sunlight comforts me.

I like to sleep with the window open.

MY STORY

These pages reflect your background. Let others know about your childhood, the good and bad. We react emotionally to what we remember. Emotional scars and abuse can lead to behaviors and it is important that caregivers know if there are any issues. In each section I have included some examples to get you started and some space at the end for any additional thoughts.

I grew up (on a farm/in a small town/in the city).
My house was (describe your house).

When I was a child I loved to visit:

When I was a child, I liked to:

As a child, I remember loving to eat/hating to eat.
I still do/do not like to eat this.

I remember being afraid of:

I remember counting the days until I could see or go to

What did your parents do for a living? What is/was your occupation?

Add more thoughts here:

NEIGHBORHOOD

Today's culture leads us to stay to ourselves and not talk to our neighbor's much. In this section define what your neighborhood was like growing up and presently.

Share about where you were born and when. What was the general feeling in America at that time?

Describe your neighborhood. Was it close knit and with block parties or did everybody mind their own business.

Describe your neighbors? Were there bakers on the block?   Was there a handyman that fixed things for everyone?

Was there a neighborhood bully? Describe him or her and how they affected you.

Did the neighbors of your childhood affect how you speak with your neighbors now?

Share anything else you like.

EDUCATION

Our school experiences do a lot to shape our personality. I met my best friend in high school and enjoyed spending time there.

Did you like school? Why/Why not? Did you earn a degree?

Write down your thoughts about special clubs, activities, and favorite subjects.

Describe your favorite school memories.

Did you do well in school or was it a struggle to graduate?

What did you study in college or trade school, or, if you didn't go, what did you want to study?

Any other thoughts or feelings to share?

FAMILY

OK, let's talk about your family and childhood next.
Were you close knit or did you fight a lot, or both.

Talk about your relationship you're your siblings, now and as you were growing up.

Describe your pets.

Talk about any jobs or chores you had growing up. Did they influence your educational decisions?

Describe the relationship between yours parents and their parents and siblings.

Add any memories or stories here.

ADULT YEARS

Now that we have gotten through childhood let's move on to adulthood. Use this page to talk about marriages and children. Home life and traditions during this time can also be included here.

Discuss your wedding, honeymoon and favorite memories of the occasion.

Describe your children and/or nieces and nephews. Add any thoughts on other children you were close to.

How is your children's current relationship with you and their siblings? Can you describe a defining moment that may have changed their relationship?

How long were/are you married? Were you married more than once? Was there any illness, accidents, or any other events, good or bad, that changed your marriage? If you can, include any domestic violence issues that impacted you. What form did it take? How did you handle adversity? Domestic Violence issues impact those with memory loss greatly. If there are behavioral issues or fear it could be because of this experience.

Talk about your career and your feelings about it.
Did you enjoy your work or was it just a job?

What did your retirement look like? Were you a world traveler or did you stay home with the grandkids. Describe a time when someone made you feel important after retirement.

Who were the people who have impacted you the most and why?

Let's end this chapter with your personal insights on your life to this point. What generally makes you happy or sad?

Do you consider yourself successful? Why or why not?

Are you a social person or are you happy in your home by yourself with your cat?

How do you feel about growing older? Anything you would change or have regrets about?

What are your current hobbies, fears and pet peeves?

Do you have a personal philosophy you would like to share?

Do you have any items on your bucket list that are unfulfilled?

I have added some space for any other thoughts not mentioned here that would go along with this chapter.

HEALTH AND LIFESTYLE

Do you consider yourself a healthy person? The next two categories are for your current health needs and medications. I left plenty of room to update as needed. You might want to use pencil here or indicate updates by date.

Who is your primary care physician?

What are your current health issues,
Diagnoses?_____

_____

_____

_____

_____

_____

_____

_____

_____

_____

_____

_____

_____

What current medications are you taking?

_____

_____

_____

_____

_____

_____

_____

_____

_____

_____

_____

_____

_____

_____

Let folks know about your nutrition preferences on this page. Do you have any allergies or special dietary needs?

What are your sleep habits? Maybe you had a job where you had to work nights so you are used to sleeping during the day.

Do you partake in any exercise? Maybe you and your dog took a stroll every morning or you were a marathon runner.

Is there anything that causes you stress?

Are there certain things or situations that you find embarrassing?

How would you describe yourself as a person?

What are your hobbies? Did you ever collect anything?

What do you like or dislike on TV? Do you have a favorite show? Do you enjoy a good western or musical?

What kind of music do you like?

What books do you like to read?

Do you like sports? Which ones? What is your favorite team or type of sport that you like to watch on TV?

Use this space for describing anything that you feel describes your down time and stress relieving activities.

TRAVEL

Maybe your idea of travel is a good TV episode of Survivor or Lost. Some folks have a career where they get to travel. Are you one of those folks that likes to plan every minute, or would you prefer to just go find a beach somewhere and live on it for a week.

Where have you traveled? Where would you like to go, but have never been?

Do you like cruises? Why or why not? Have you been on any?

Where do your relatives live and how often did you visit?

Talk about your leisure visits. Do you enjoy skiing, the beach, fine dining or just puttering around the house?

Any more thoughts on travel you wish to share?

ANXIETIES, FEARS AND PHOBIAS

Being unable to speak for yourself can be unnerving by itself. Adding other stressors can really let loose your frontal lobe barriers. Take this time to talk about the things that make you anxious. I know one person who said she didn't like her face touched. Really think about what would make you flip out. On the other hand, if the signals were mixed and you got upset, what would relax you? Do you like lots of natural light, flowers, music? Maybe some ice cream. Do you like to be read to? Some folks like art therapy, things like coloring, drawing and painting.

I have a fear of _____. Do you know why you have this fear? What sets it off?

I get anxious around _____.

How do you feel around holidays? Describe any mood changes.

Is there a certain type of music that immediately relaxes you?

What is your favorite flower and why?

Are there certain types of people that make you anxious or mad?

What else make you anxious?

SPIRITUAL

Your Spiritual journey is important. It is the one thing that will be there until your final breath. It is important for others to know how to help you in your final journey and what type of support to provide. Reflect on your faith.

Do you attend church or other place of worship? If so, where do you attend?

Are you still involved in your church? If not, what are the barriers for you?

Did you volunteer anywhere? What did you enjoy about it?

Describe your feelings about death.

What, if any, religious holidays have meaning to you?

What is your belief system? How do you foresee your end of life? Describe it here.

EMOTIONS

Do you cry at a sappy commercial? This page should reflect your emotions. What makes you happy and sad? Glad and mad? How do you handle anger?

Is there a color that is calming to you? What about a type of music?

Are there certain types of clothing that make you happy? Maybe a favorite blanket,

Add your thoughts here.

LIKES AND DISLIKES

FOOD

Which one of us hasn't been comforted by food at some point? Of course, we don't want to throw a plate on the floor in frustration or refuse to eat because we are given something we absolutely hate. Use this page to describe what you love and hate to eat. Personally, I hate spicy but I have a friend that lives for salsa. Are you drawn to things sweet or salty? Do you prefer desserts, vegetables, or both? List everything you can think of. I don't want to limit you here so I have left blank space for your thoughts. Beverages can fit in this category too. Are you a coffee drinker or do you like tea? How do you take them? What about a diet coke? Here are some ideas.

My choice of condiments

I like my potatoes

    Mashed, baked, tater, French fries

Ice cream flavor;

Favorite dessert;

Favorite restaurant

ENTERTAINMENT

What makes you happy? Think about what you like to do on your day off or after a busy work day.

What section of the newspaper do you prefer?

What did you enjoy watching when you were younger?

Are you an opera fan? Musicals?

What type or types of movies do you prefer and do you have a favorite?

What sort of books do you like?

Did you have a membership to the zoo or the art museum or maybe the amusement park? Describe it and how often you went.

What's the one song that's going to make you get up and punch the wall?

What song reminds you of family?

Other thoughts?

PERSONAL AND HYGIENE

Here's a stinky subject. Personal hygiene is probably the biggest reason for behavior issues with those who are not able to express their needs. Letting folks know ahead of time what your preferences are is a great way to keep everyone safe and content.

Do you prefer showers or baths and what time of day?

Did you paint your nails? What color?

Do you like fluffy pillows or ones that are flat?

Do you like lots of blankets or just a sheet?

What kind of hairstyle do you prefer?

Use this space to talk about clothing preferences and colors.

THE FINAL JOURNEY

So, your caregivers, family and friends have followed your wishes to this point and managed to keep you happy. You are preparing for your final journey. This is the most difficult part for your caregivers so let's help them out here as well. This may be the most important piece of the puzzle. Take time to think about what you want here. Do you want someone in the room with you when you are actively dying? I hear so many stories of folks saying that they were with Mom around the clock and they left the room for a minute and that's when she passed. In fact, Mom was just waiting for that moment alone.

Is it important for you to be at home or just surrounded by the things you love?

What kind of final arrangements do you want? If you have already prepared your plan, where would this information be (funeral home, friend, relative, etc.)?

If you are planning a burial is there a favorite outfit you want to wear or an item you would like to have with you?

Have you had any positive experiences with death you want to share?

ADVANCED DIRECTIVES

Advanced Directives are written orders telling family, medical staff and others your wishes for end of life care. They are an important part of your story. They are an indicator of how you want your final journey to begin. Do you want to fight it all the way or just let nature take its course? Maybe it's something in between.

Here are the documents you need.

Power of Attorney for Health Care

- This documents names an agent to make decisions on your behalf. There are three main types. A General Power of Attorney is comprehensive and covers all decision making. They would be acting as if they are you, even in financial matters. The Durable Power of Attorney is general or limited in scope and can take effect the minute you sign it, if you wish it too, and remains effective even when you become incapacitated. A Springing Power of Attorney is only good when you become incapacitated and a doctor deems you incompetent. It gives the doctors guidance on who the decision maker for your care is when you are unable to state your wishes. Make sure you choose an agent for your Power of Attorney that will make decisions the way you want things to be. If your spouse is adamant about doing everything possible to keep you alive but you want the plugs pulled, then don't choose him or her.

Living Wills

Providing a living will gives written guidance about your wishes to your agent with power of attorney. If you don't want a feeding tube, you can indicate it on this form and that makes it easier for your power of attorney.

Do Not Resuscitate Order

This written order is for the special case where emergency personnel have come to your aid and you have no pulse. If you have this on your refrigerator with a current picture and the EMT's are called, they will know to not try and revive you. You can get these documents on the internet, (search for Advanced Directives and whatever state you live in), through an estate planning attorney or through an organization called Aging with Dignity. For a nominal fee, you can complete all the documents on their website at www.agingwithdignity.org.

That's it you're done. You did a great job and your caregiver will appreciate the work you have done and how they can look forward to a better relationship with you.

ACKNOWLEDGMENTS

I would like to express my gratitude to the many people I have talked to and taken care of in my lifetime. They are the inspirations for this book. The many caregivers who struggled and cried, the care recipients who attempted to communicate their needs when they had no voice. This book is for them.

My thanks to all those who volunteered the examples given throughout this book. Their insights helped me to form the specific chapters and thoughts throughout.

A very special thanks to Dr. Robert Parsons, who took time out of his already busy life to edit these pages.

I hope that all who write their thoughts here and those that read about the lives of their loved ones will be comforted by these pages.